Puzzle Me

Brain Ticklers

By Kris Vaicikonis

BRIGHT
connections media™

A World Book Encyclopedia Company

Bright Connections Media
A World Book Encyclopedia Company
233 North Michigan Avenue
Chicago, Illinois 60601
U.S.A.

For information about other BCM publications,
visit our website at http://www.brightconnectionsmedia.com
or call 1-800-967-5325.

Puzzle Me: Brain Ticklers
ISBN: 978-1-62267-005-5

Printed in China by Toppan Leefung Printing Ltd.,
Guangdong Province
1st printing July 2012

Acknowledgments

Front and back cover: © Simon Greig, Shutterstock; © Michael Jung,
Shutterstock; © Wavebreak Media/Thinkstock; © Tischenko Irina,
Shutterstock; © blue67design/Shutterstock

Interior: WORLD BOOK illustrations; © Shutterstock

TABLE OF CONTENTS

Where's Stella?

The children's dog, Stella, is lost in the middle of the lumberyard! Can you show them which path they have to take to find her?

answer on page 28

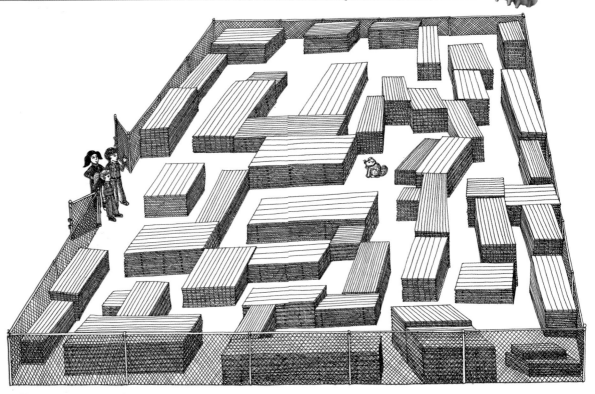

4

The last acorn

For weeks, Sammy Squirrel and his friend Tammy have been gathering acorns. Now, there is only one acorn left. Can you show Sammy which branch leads to the acorn? And remember, it's not fair to jump from one branch to another!

answer on page 28

5

Which balloon?

Victoria has just bought a balloon. The monkey is handing her the string. Which balloon is attached to the string?

answer on page 28

Rhyming pairs

On this page there are five pairs of things whose names rhyme. Can you match each pair?

Ladybugs, ladybugs!

Which two ladybugs look exactly alike?

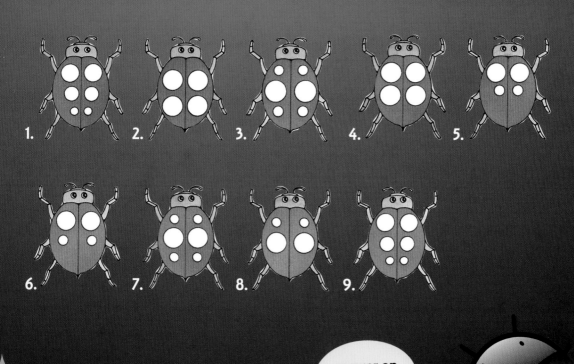

answer on page 28

8

Ollie the Octopus

Which shadow exactly matches Ollie's picture?

1.   2.   3.

4.   5.   6.

answer on page 29

What's different?

The pictures on this page seem to be just the same. But if you look closely, you will see that they are not. Some of the things in the top picture (a) are missing from the bottom picture (b). Can you find what things are missing?

a

b

answer on page 29

Mixed-up snakes

One of these five snakes is different from all the others. Can you find it?

answer
on
page 29

Rebus

A rebus is a puzzle in which pictures, letters, and numbers stand for words. In some cases, you must subtract a letter from a word, or from the name of an object, to get the right word. This rebus contains three words that mean a lot to everyone.

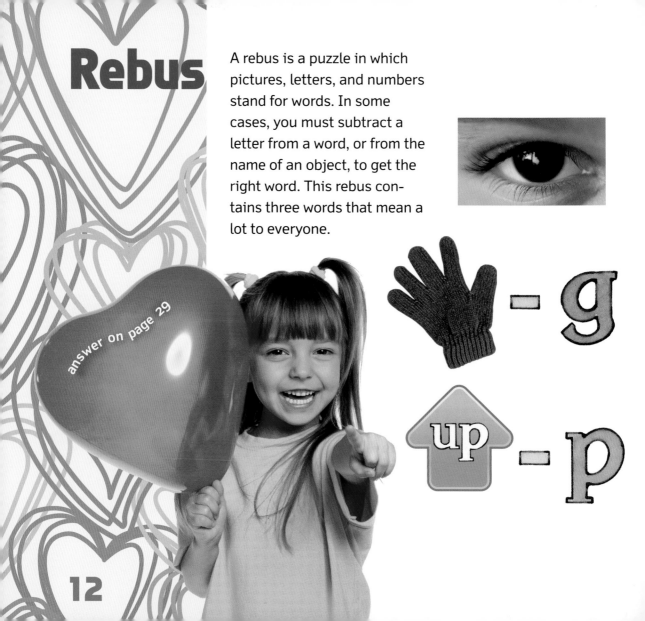

answer on page 29

Picture-words

The first letters in the names of the objects in each row can be put together to make a word. When the three words are put together, they make a sentence. What is the sentence?

answer on page 29

Joke riddles

The answers to these riddles really don't make much sense. But they're funny!

Why does a bear have a fur coat?

Because it would look silly in a raincoat.

Why were ancient Egyptian boys and girls such good children?

Because they respected their mummies.

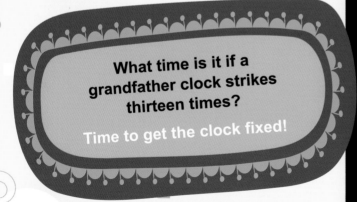

What time is it if a grandfather clock strikes thirteen times?

Time to get the clock fixed!

14

What does an envelope say when it's licked?

It just shuts up and doesn't say anything.

Why isn't it a good idea to go for a walk on an empty stomach?

Because it's easier to walk on a sidewalk.

What's the longest word in the dictionary?

Smile— there's a mile after the first letter.

Which is faster, heat or cold?

Heat, because you can catch cold.

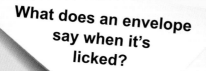

Why was the little raspberry crying?

Because its mom and dad were in a jam.

What bus once crossed an ocean?

Colum-bus.

What animal can jump higher than a mountain?

Any animal. A mountain can't jump!

What has a hundred legs, but can't walk a single step?

Fifty pairs of pants.

Why do birds fly south for the winter?

Because it's too far to walk.

Why did the little girl think that the cook was mean?

She saw him beating eggs and whipping cream.

Name six things that have milk in them.

Ice cream, cocoa, pudding, and three cows.

Why did the little boy take a ruler to bed with him?

Because he wanted to find out how long he was asleep.

17

The spilled ice cream

Arrange two toothpicks and a large coin or button as shown on the right.

Think of this shape as an ice-cream cone with one scoop of ice cream in it. Can you move one toothpick so that the ice-cream cone is upside down and the ice cream (the button) is no longer inside the cone?

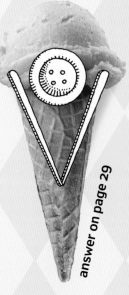

answer on page 29

Ice-cream sundae

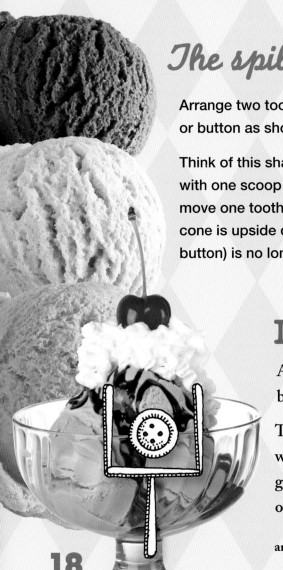

Arrange four toothpicks and a small button or coin as shown on the left.

This is an ice-cream sundae glass with a cherry in it! Can you turn the glass upside down and get the cherry out by moving only two toothpicks?

answer on page 29

House into squares

Using six toothpicks, make a "house" as shown on the left.

Now, moving only two toothpicks, change the "house" into five squares.

answer on page 30

Triangle turnaround

Using buttons or coins, set up a triangle like the one shown here. Then, by moving only *three* of the buttons, see if you can turn the whole triangle around to face the other way, with the point at the bottom!

answer on page 30

Can it be done?

1. It's easy to arrange fifteen buttons in five rows with three buttons in each row. But can you arrange seven buttons in five rows with three buttons in each row?

answer on page 30

2. It's easy to arrange twenty buttons in five rows with four buttons in each row. But can you arrange ten buttons in five rows with four buttons in each row?

A trip downtown

Shayla and her mother went downtown. They rode the bus, because Shayla's father had taken the car to work. They visited a doctor and saw a movie about dinosaurs at the museum.

Shayla's father does not go to work on Saturday or Sunday. The doctor's office is closed on Wednesday. The bus they took makes mid-day runs only on Monday, Wednesday, Friday, and Saturday. The museum shows a different movie on Friday. What day did Shayla and her mother go downtown?

answer on page 30

Ginny and Sarah

Sarah is now the same age that Ginny was four years ago. Four years ago, Ginny was twice as old as Sarah. Ginny is now twelve. How old is Sarah?

answer on page 31

Black and white kittens

Marilyn's cat has had a litter of kittens. Some are all black and some are all white. Each black kitten has the same number of white brothers and sisters as black ones.

But each white kitten has twice as many black brothers and sisters as white ones. How many kittens are in the litter?

answer on page 31

The great mouse race

answer on page 31

Wheep, Squee, Eeper, Tweep, and Pweet are mice. Like all mice, they are fast runners. One day, the five mice decided to hold a race to see who was the fastest. When the race was over, here is how they finished:

* Wheep was not first.
* Pweet finished right behind Wheep.
* Squee was not second.
* Eeper came in two places after Squee.
* Tweep was not first or last.

Can you figure out the order in which the mice finished the race?

The new kids

A new family had moved into the neighborhood. When Mrs. Frisby, a neighbor, passed the house, she saw four children playing in the yard. She could tell they were brothers and sisters, for they all looked very much alike.

"My, what a nice, big family," she exclaimed. "What are your names and ages?"

answer on page 31

"I'm Carl," said a boy. He pointed at a girl who stood beside him. This is Jennifer. I'm a year older than she is."

"I'm George," said another boy. "I'm a year younger than my sister Susie."

"I'll be eight next month," announced Jennifer. "I'm three years younger than Susie."

How old was each child?

All kinds of codes

Here are some secret messages to decode. Once you have figured out how each code works, you can use it with your friends.

answer on page 32

1. In this message, numbers are obviously used for letters. Here is a hint: Everything is in the proper order.

4 5 3 15 4 9 14 7 9 19 6 21 14

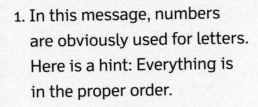

2. Look very carefully at this message:

ITI SALLIN HO WYO
ULOO KATIT

3. The clue for this message is: *backwards.*

GSV ZOKSZYVG RH
GFIMVW ZILFMW

4. This one is much harder, because you have to decode it twice. After you decode it once, look at it carefully.

HKZ XVWW RUUV IVMGO BZMWYZ
XPDZ IWH

Answers

Where's Stella? (page 4)

The last acorn (page 5)

Which balloon? (page 6)

Rhyming pairs (page 7)

goat—boat

book—cook

fish—dish

tree—key

mouse—house

Ladybugs, ladybugs! (page 8)

Numbers 1 and 9 are the same.

Ollie the Octopus (page 9)

Ollie's shadow is number 5.

What's different? (page 10)

In picture b, the trees on the left are missing, the horse's spots are reversed, the squirrel is facing the opposite direction, the fence is missing a rail, and the blue butterflies are missing.

Mixed-up snakes
(page 11)

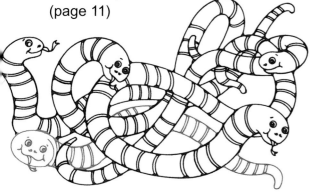

Rebus (page 12)

I love you

Picture-words (page 13)

helicopter, owl, windmill:	how
apple, rhinoceros, egg:	are
yo-yo, ostrich, umbrella:	you

The spilled ice cream (page 18)

To turn the cone upside down, simply move one of the toothpicks to the right (or left), as shown.

Ice-cream sundae (page 18)

To turn the glass upside down, first slide the horizontal toothpick over, as shown in (B) below. Then move the leftover toothpick to form the other side of the glass, as shown in (C).

House into squares (page 19)

Move the two toothpicks that form the roof so as to make a cross inside the square, as shown. This makes four small squares inside one large square, or a total of five squares.

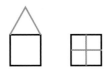

Can it be done? (page 21)

1. Arrange the seven buttons as shown at right. This gives you five rows of three buttons, as shown by the blue lines.

2. Arrange the ten buttons as shown. This gives you five rows of four buttons, as shown by the blue lines.

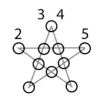

Triangle turnaround (page 20)

Move the end buttons on the bottom row to the second row. Move the button that's on top to the bottom.

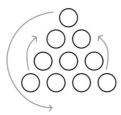

A trip downtown (page 22)

Shayla's father does not work downtown on Saturday or Sunday. We know he was at work on this day, so Saturday and Sunday are ruled out. The doctor's office is closed on Wednesday, so Wednesday is out. The bus that Shayla and her mother want to take does not run in the middle of the day on Tuesday and Thursday, so these days are out. The museum does not show the dinosaur movie on Friday, but that is the movie Shayla and her mother saw. So, Friday is ruled out. This leaves only Monday.

Ginny and Sarah (page 22)

Ginny is now twelve. Four years ago, she was eight. If Sarah is now the same age Ginny was four years ago, Sarah is now eight.

Black and white kittens (page 23)

There are seven kittens in the litter—four black and three white. Each black kitten has three black and three white brothers and sisters. Each white kitten has two white and four black brothers and sisters.

The great mouse race (page 24)

We know that Wheep was not first. Pweet finished right behind Wheep, so she could not have been first, either. Eeper came in two places after Squee, so obviously he was not first. And Tweep was neither first nor last. That leaves only Squee. Squee was the winner.

If Squee was first, and we know that Eeper came in two places after her, then Eeper must have come in third.

We know that Pweet finished right behind Wheep. If Wheep had finished second, that would mean that Pweet had finished third. But from what we have worked out, we know that Eeper was third. So, Wheep could not have come in second. He had to have come in fourth. And, if Pweet was behind him, she must have been fifth. Tweep, then, had to have been second.

So, the order of finish in the Great Mouse Race was:

1. Squee 2. Tweep 3. Eeper
4. Wheep 5. Pweet

The new kids (page 25)

Jennifer announced that she would be eight next month, which means she is now seven. So, if she's three years younger than Susie, Susie is ten. Carl said he was a year older than Jennifer, so he is eight. And George, who is a year younger than Susie, must be nine.

All kinds of codes (page 26)

1. Numbers are used for letters in proper alphabetical order. Thus, 1 is A, 2 is B, and so on. So, the message reads:

    4 5 3 15   4 9 14 7   9 19   6 21 14

    D E C O D I N G   I S   F U N

2. If you looked carefully, you saw that the message is made up of ordinary words that are just spaced differently:

    ITI SALLIN HO WYO ULOO KATIT

    IT IS ALL IN HOW YOU LOOK AT IT

3. The letters of the alphabet have been turned around so that A is Z, B is Y, and so on:

    GSV ZOKSZYVG RH GFIMVW ZILFMW

    THE ALPHABET IS TURNED AROUND

4. If you realized that this, too, is a backwards alphabet, as in (3), you decoded it and got:

    HKZ XVWW RUUV IVMGO BZMWYZ XPZD   IWH

    SPA   CEDD   IFFE   RENTL YANDBA CKWA RDS

    Then, if you looked at it carefully, as the clue suggested, you saw that it was just ordinary words spaced differently, as in (2).

    SPA CEDD IFFE RENTL YANDBA CKWA RDS

    SPACED   DIFFERENTLY AND BACKWARDS